# Red Stones

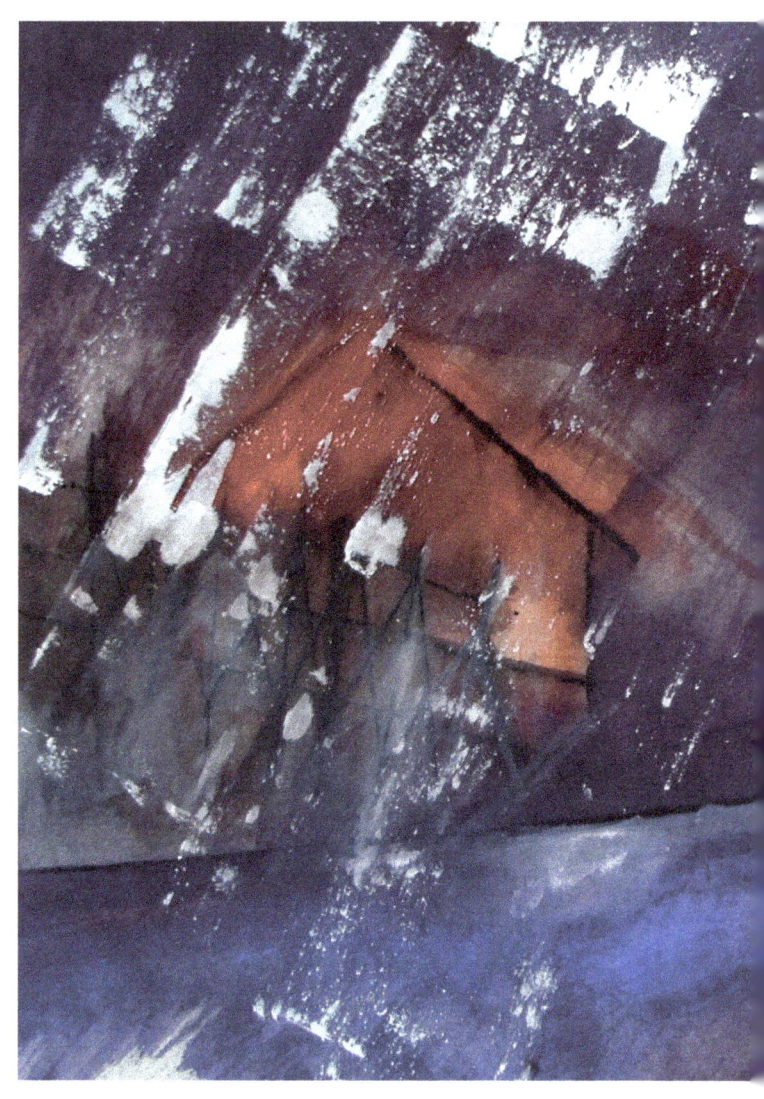

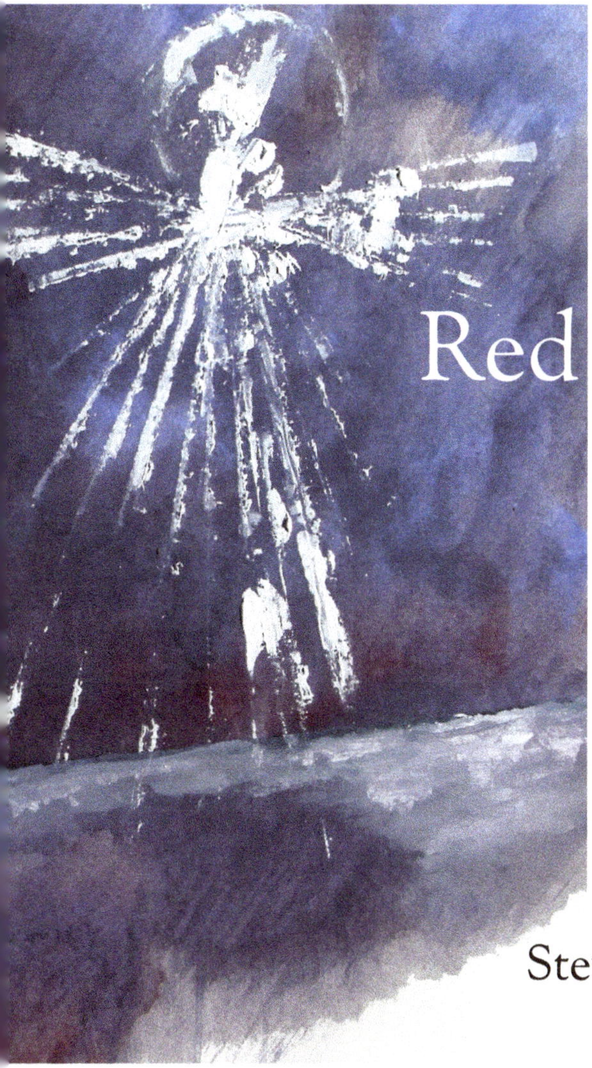

# Red Stones

Jonas Zdanys
*poems*

Steven Schroeder
*paintings*

Lamar University Literary Press

Poems Copyright © 2016 Jonas Zdanys, all rights reserved
Paintings Copyright © 2016 Steven Schroeder, all rights reserved

ISBN: 978-1-942956-21-1
Library of Congress Control Number: 2016934217

ACKNOWLEDGMENTS
Poems I – XXV originally appeared as a limited edition letterpress chapbook titled *Cormorants* published by Timberline Press, with all paper-making, printing and binding done at the Boston Paper Collective in Charlestown, Massachusetts. Poems II, III and XXIII appeared as "The Abrasions of Rain/雨水的磨損" in English, and in Chinese translation by Chris Song Zijiang, in *Wonderbook of Poetry*, published in Macau. Poems II, III, IX, XIII, XIV, XV, XVI, XIX, XXIII, and XXX appeared as Lithuanian versions in *Literatūra ir Menas* (n. 45), published in Vilnius. Poems XXXVII, XXXVIII, and XXXIX were published as "from The Homilies of Prester John" in *all roads will lead you home* (September 2014). I am most grateful to Sacred Heart University for granting me faculty release time to work on this collection and on other volumes.
JZ

A list of image titles appears at the end of the text.

Design by Regina Schroeder / forgetgutenberg.com

Manufactured in the United States of America

Lamar University Literary Press
Beaumont, Texas

## Recent Poetry from Lamar University Literary Press

Charles Behlen, *Failing Heaven*
Jerry Bradley, *Crownfeathers and Effigies*
Jerry Bradley & Ulf Kirchdorfer (eds), *The Great American Wise Ass Poetry Anthology*
Matthew Brennan, *One Life*
Paul Christensen, *The Jack of Diamonds is a Hard Card to Play*
Chip Dameron, *Waiting for an Etcher*
William Virgil Davis, *The Bones Poems*
Michelle Hartman, *Irony and Irreverence*
Katherine Hoerth, *Goddess Wears Cowboy Boots*
Lynn Hoggard, *Motherland*
Ulf Kirchdorfer, *Chewing Green Leaves*
Laozi, *Daodejing*, tr. by David Breeden, Steven Schroeder, & Wally Swist
Erin Murphy, *Ancilla*
Laurence Musgrove, *Local Bird*
Kornelijus Platelis, *Solitary Architectures*
Jan Seale, *The Parkinson Poems*
Steven Schroeder, *the moon, not the finger, pointing*
Carol Smallwood, *Water, Earth, Air, Fire, and Picket Fences*
Glen Sorestad, *Hazards of Eden*
W.K. Stratton, *Ranchero Ford/ Dying in Red Dirt Country*
Wally Swist, *Invocation*
Jonas Zdanys (ed.), *Pushing the Envelope, Epistolary Poems*

For information on these and other
Lamar University Literary Press books go to
www.Lamar.edu/literarypress

## *Selected Books By Jonas Zdanys*

### Poems in English

*Cormorants*, 2013
*The Kingfisher's Reign*, 2012
*The Thin Light of Winter*, 2009
*Salt*, 2007
*The Woman on the Bridge*, 2005
*The White City*, 2004
*White*, 2004
*Lithuanian Crossing*, 1999
*Water Light*, 1997
*Priam's Daughter*, 1997
*The White Bend of the River*, 1994
*The Metaphysics of Wolves*, 1994
*Maine Aubade*, 1990
*Voice on an Anthill*, 1982

### Poems in Lithuanian

*Ikaro prisikėlimas*, 2014
*Tarpdury*, 2008
*Dūmų stulpai*, 2002
*Dotnuvos stoty*, 1999
*Aušros Daina*, 1993

## Contents

I / 1
*The wind stirs under the back stairs*
II / 2
*The mind is a still distraction*
III / 3
*The short breath of night runs shallow*
IV / 4
*Darkness sets cold against the wall*
V / 5
*The stars in the sky have been dead*
VI / 8
*Lone Woman of San Nicolas*
VII / 9
*There are nights when the moon rises*
VIII / 10
*The day is a discarded stick*
IX / 11
*Snow falls cold and thick in the fields*
X / 12
*Bent gray figures in the thin grass*
XI / 13
*Evening falls to the cool silence*
XII / 15
*This is marshland and undercreek*
XIII / 16
*Winter came as the chestnuts fell*

XIV / 17
*Morning was unconcerned as fog*
XV / 18
*It was the place where time ended*
XVI / 19
*We moved at last toward the flat banks*
XVII / 20
*The buried day unhinged itself*
XVIII / 21
*The present fades away slowly*
XIX / 23
*I have learned at last what love is*
XX / 24
*This thing can come to life again*
XXI / 25
*We must be diligent today*
XXII / 26
*We are ghosts when we see what ghosts*
XXIII / 27
*I measure the passage of time*
XXIV / 28
*Green water flows in place of blood*
XXV / 29
*The bridges and streets are patterns*
XXVI / 30
*I have learned to sit silent and alone*
XXVII / 31
*When the dead thrash in the pale east*

XXVIII / 34
*She held the dry grass in her hand*
XXIX / 35
*The yellow essence of summer*
XXX / 36
*When the music stops, when the wide-winged*
XXXI / 37
*The least motion, the vulnerable descent*
XXXII / 38
*I reach no conclusions*
XXXIII / 39
*It was an artificial light*
XXXIV / 40
*The well-lit room with two yellow vases*
XXXV / 41
*I woke late in the empty house*
XXXVI / 42
*The responsibility of love realized*
XXXVII / 43
*It was when the last bird flew by the window*
XXXVIII / 46
*The stolen hours carried him beyond the lands*
XXXIX / 47
*Fish and flocks, the unsummoned image*
XL / 48
*The certain solitudes of the blood moon*
XLI / 49
*We stepped across the broken glass*

XLII / 50
*The indifferent night writes an old history*
XLIII / 52
*Snow falls on old statues in the square*
XLIV / 53
*We each close a door to a small room*
XLV / 54
*Day at last turns into night*
XLVI / 56
*Those old things that filled the room*
XLVII / 57
*Endless clouds of smoke fill the horizon*
XLVIII / 58
*A heavy vine of wings covers the stones*
XLIX / 60
*An abandoned child sleeps alone*
L / 61
*The weather changes, separating shadow and light*
LI / 62
*The curve around the bend in the road*
LII / 64
*At the other edge of the field, toward the end of May*
LIII / 65
*The rage of summer fires in the distance*
LIV / 66
*Winter is hanging on, a cold fire*
LV / 67
*Evening offers no relief. The incandescence*

LVI / 68
*The broken boxes the moon fell into last night*
LVII / 69
*The rituals of time mock the rigid stars*
LVIII / 71
*The private certainties of time, when the tide*
LIX / 72
*The last white leaf on the birch tree as the storm passes*
LX / 73
*The river gathered itself quickly near the fallen trees*

Afterword: Notes on the Paintings and Poems

I

The wind stirs under the back stairs,
drifts across a transparent dark
where nothing begins, nothing ends.
The day gives form to scattered dust.
The present is an open door
in the hours of a broken room.
Muted voices hover above
the revelations of old walls.
Stars lift on a bent horizon.
Gaunt birds above the tiled clay roof,
wings angled in a feathered cross,
sharpen the hardened edge of time.

## II

The mind is a still distraction.
The white blankets burn in pitch black
and night salts the blood of heaven.
The men at war at the turned gates
of the torn city plant their heels
among the spider webs and dirt,
not terrified of loss or death
or the hinge of mud washed across
the hesitation in their eyes.
Think of nothing. Let the body
become a pale reflection of
ancient wings in the wind's cold glass.

III

The short breath of night runs shallow
and slow across the city's streets
and rain slides, thin as hunger, on
gray diagonals of iron.
Angels made of straw, luminous
as wind in bags of vague paper,
turn their backs to the old red house.
I touch the star above the black
canal, bewildered and endless,
and the world quickens at my feet.
Beyond the square, the lost dogs bark
the secret names of fire and ice.

IV

Darkness sets cold against the wall.
I open the shuttered windows,
lights crowded in the graying panes,
and the brilliance of the year
comes to its full circle, recurs
in the instant that penetrates
the heart as the day moves to its
radiant decline. The air lifts
and the stars drift down as night falls
absolved by the brittle eclipse
of white shadows on black water
and the passing of time to clay.

V

The stars in the sky have been dead
for a thousand years, their slow shades
absorbing the last night until
the present moment, consonant
and urgent, is at last reversed
and our lives are renewed again
in the invisible season.
Every hour has its true color,
every minute its note and breath—
our last necessities whispered
on our search for eternity's
blue dream paling in a flat land.

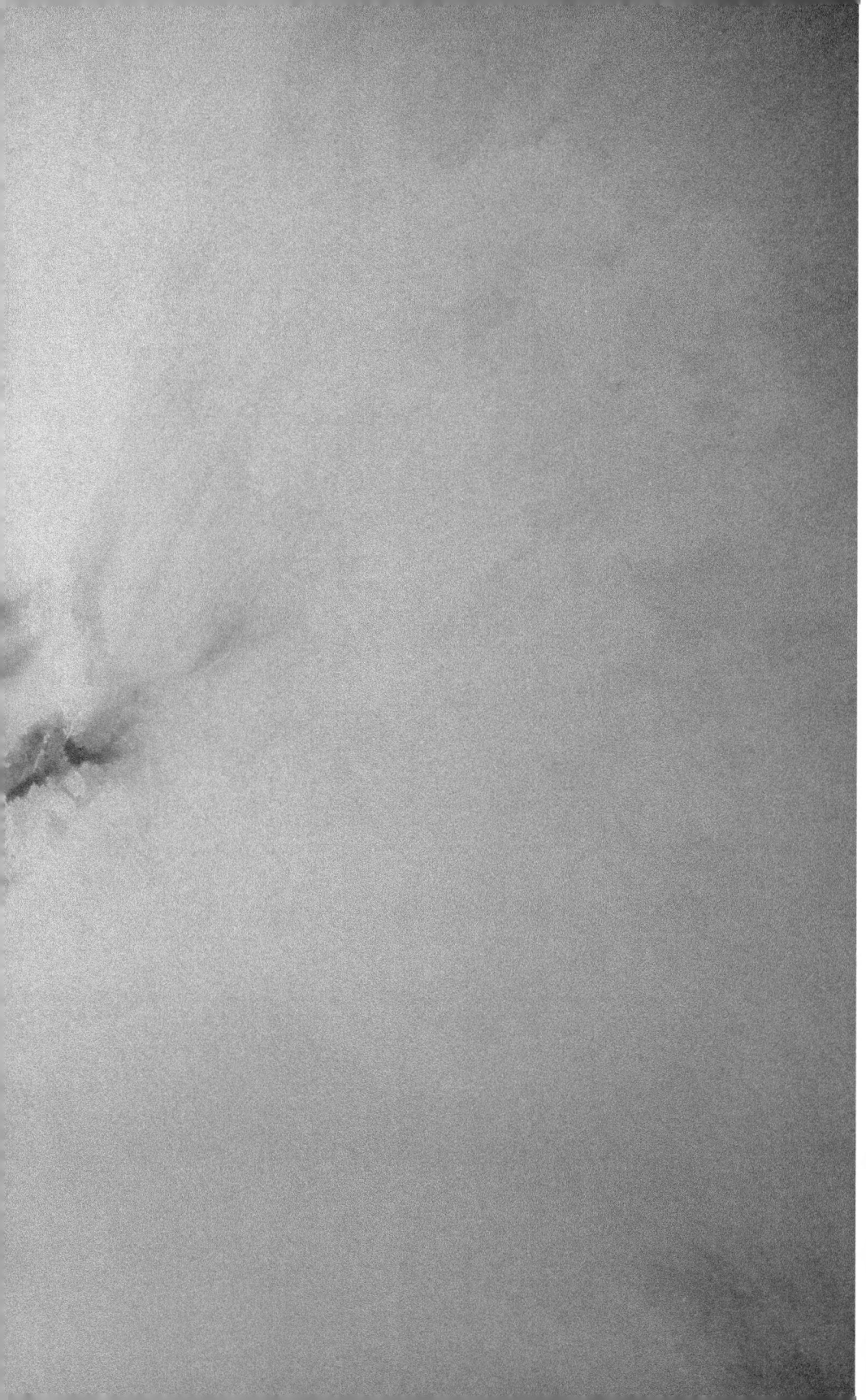

## VI

Lone Woman of San Nicolas,
the ashen feathers of your dress,
torn loose from their strings of sinew,
float down across the southern coast
of ancient California.
Flowers in a distant meadow
the artifice of truth and light.
The flat roads of autumn count out
the tallies of a world in gray
that spins across the universe
as birds of Santa Barbara
drift low above your unmarked grave.

## VII

There are nights when the moon rises
and the air is comfortable
and slow, and the late stars thicken
high above the far horizon,
and the ache of moving water
circles to things thin as smoke and
tipped with flame across the heavens.
These echoes of the infinite
held in the voices of others,
the language of gods and children.
You gaze far out, and when you wake
and lift your head, the world is you.

## VIII

The day is a discarded stick
in the ruins of the garden,
the outline of a worn silence,
wordless and alone, that traces
the edges of the first real night,
ambitious and blind as dried weeds,
to the shape of an ash gray bird
in the branches of an old tree.
Conscience wakes despair: the three notes
they heard were a call to death of
the universe of old knowledge,
the world's history pulsed away.

## IX

Snow falls cold and thick in the fields
of asphodel, pale meadows near
the margins of a pallid sea.
Waves break on the dying embers
of afternoon, the blank corners
of the sky waking at twilight
to spare colors and the hollow
pausings of ice among the stones:
an inexorable world where
the lamentations of gray ghosts
gutter above the empty plains
and narrow orbits of our lives.

X

Bent gray figures in the thin grass
scythe the earth near the fragile edge
of land along the water where
dry spaces turn to root and air.
The day flows down the deep river,
the sky whole and undivided,
the world brittle as withered leaves
in a thick stand of white birches.
There is a source of constant light.
I watch them take wing like shadows
on a crest of easy failure,
turn and sing testaments to night.

## XI

Evening falls to the cool silence
of silver willows and slow fish,
the cries of fishermen and gulls
that float across the water to
outlines of possibility
and the narrow order of grace
glowing like new fire in the sky.
Small bells ring above the old boats
as light slowly washes away.
The image returns to itself:
the white moon pausing in the wind
as weary as the dead must be.

## XII

This is marshland and undercreek,
the place of sleep where birds breathe their
first and last, where darkness and heat
along the edges of water
settle in the long yellow grass
and in the cold curved light of dreams,
where twilight deepens downriver
and autumn crests, pleating to bone.
We watch infinity open
and close the veiled wind in the trees,
and the three day rain crowds away
past this and that other country.

XIII

Winter came as the chestnuts fell
and stars arched up from the bottom
of the world, winking at the cold.
The last bird across the river
made a small sound in the dark, like
a far wind crying in vigil
or woe out past the dry roadside
dotted with hawkweed gone to seed,
deepened beyond recognition.
Deliver me from this fragile
interruption, let my body
rise once more to silence and light.

## XIV

Morning was unconcerned as fog.
The long walk in transparent rain,
the climb through violet shadows
shaped like birds above blunt water
far off in a gasping of air.
The momentum of naked grass,
the old lie of earth above earth
and stones that shift in endless chains
to the inarticulate sound
of heaven past the triple wall,
the broken branch that grows again
death's tangent on the horizon.

## XV

It was the place where time ended,
the pale drawn shade of history,
as gathered as a sudden dream,
no longer present or past but
open and splendid with quick knives.
The year ends with patches of red
on the water and hands that reach
far beyond the isolation
of the world, fleeting bone that bends
to air and whispers to itself
in the eternal moment that
cusps the last rising of the moon.

## XVI

We moved at last toward the flat banks,
our voices thick with mud and haze.
I heard the young woman singing
across the transparent water,
smoke in the distance on the lake,
and the whisperings of others
as the moon rose in filaments
and bars of light that swarmed the clouds.
She made a sound I had never
heard before: a free soul rising
through the white season on the edge
of God's long journey filled with stars.

## XVII

The buried day unhinged itself,
flowering into an eye closed
at the center of a circle.
Afterwards, on a strip of land
that dulled against the horizon,
I came whispering with lost leaves
on the white water, came rising
into the sweet air, came gliding
out of the deep bones of the wind
unafraid, both spirit and flesh,
touching the glory overhead.
And I am here, am everywhere.

XVIII

The present fades away slowly,
the last geese crossing the edges
of the lake as the light cries out
in its own slow death and the grass
turns white and bends its own last way.
I touch the shadow of water,
live quiet as a widowed god
or marked bird in a far corner
of a universe of branches
and roots, delight in the silence
of a denser shade. My day slides
with permanence and ease to night.

## XIX

I have learned at last what love is—
black alders near ice gray water,
the abrupt single truth of air
curling the window, the blind heart
lying in wait for words and years,
the last drop of time unable
to tolerate the emptiness,
the spirit lost in lines of pain,
the bitter vacuum of low land
where a pale girl gathers flowers
with cold hands that ache forever—
and I temper myself to steel.

## XX

This thing can come to life again.
I watched slowly as shadows dipped
like a summoned vision cut loose
from the dying fire of heaven
and radiant lines of stars traced
the cold melancholy of time.
Old birds whistled among the reeds
and angled undertones of light,
their bodies transfigured to pale
winds by a moon they no longer
remember in that other place,
in that other darker season.

## XXI

We must be diligent today.
Waiting until tomorrow comes
will be too late, the arising
of form and the ending of form,
and the moment of our dying
will be unknown, every minute
grasped, the oblivion and change
to emptiness from the senses
of the body penetrated,
realized in the here and now.
Up ahead, the raft abandoned
long after we have crossed the flood.

## XXII

We are ghosts when we see what ghosts
see, when we do what ghosts do, when
we hear what only ghosts can hear.
A supple body remembered,
the metal echo of flowers
of mourning near the passing sea
where the silhouettes of birds lift
along both center and edge, hard
as the wind that cries in the dead
salt of water and stone. I hear
the glass break red in the morning,
see the mirror mindless with night.

## XXIII

I measure the passage of time
outside the smallest window with
a stick that scratches the outline
of the sickle moon on the dust
of the floor, watch a thousand years
lying gray and naked under
the wounds of the cold horizon,
count out the abrasions of rain
on the old woman's umbrella—
and understand how to endure
my longing for eternity
and the impermanence of birds.

## XXIV

Green water flows in place of blood.
Eyes of inconsolable birds
in the duckweed and dry sedges
burn with the vermillion heat
of Hesperidian apples.
The white erosion of being
gnaws the bones of heavy flowers
and the absent shadow takes hard
form at the far point of the world.
I sleep in an undiscovered
place, trapped in a pocket of air.
The season drifts, the moon slides west.

XXV

The bridges and streets are patterns
of light fragile as glass, the sky
silent with the disillusions
of the world that seep like water
into the dry sand of the years.
He had studied his life, had seen
the eye of Providence hiding
among yellow blossoms in clouds
and dust, had heard the porcelain
footsteps of angels walking through
bolted doors, had been bird and stone,
and when he turned it was the hour.

## XXVI

I have learned to sit silent and alone
as the rain falls and evening lays flat
and coarse against my skin, unbundled
to the mystery of the world.
An erratic wind in the distance abides in small
far corners, in the last dry hold of the sun.
Vulnerable things are pared thin by the moon.
The shadows of the sky slant
across the earth, tracing the outlines
of the only truths they know,
and the line cuts deep in the glass:
I see myself there, suddenly transparent.

## XXVII

When the dead thrash in the pale east
of morning as clouds strike their end,
after the door shuts and the sky
sinks green in the changing street,
after time tilts away, scraping
the bottom of each consequence,
after the recognition of the wholeness
that blinds the radiant source,
there is a sudden perfect memory
of the contradicting image,
whispers in the shadows, cold and bare,
the lost and unimaginable light.

## XXVIII

She held the dry grass in her hand,
the clarity of a long threshold
across the clusters of rain:
she put the last star to her lips,
defiant in her narrow orbit
and coveting that other world:
she pushed away the circle's shaken dust,
the synthesis of fragile patterns
that peels away the ragged form.
This is the hollow of a lost blue,
the abstraction of the moment
where the sky ends, disintegration.

## XXIX

The yellow essence of summer
at the end of the street,
ancient voices in the unlit windows,
the talking in sleep as the lights
rise in the square monotony of the sky.
How does a man die?
Quick as a broken net early in the morning
or like salt drying slowly on red rocks
washed by a late white rain?
It isn't much. It is his death.
We will grieve with the waters and sparrows.
The wings of strange birds will break with cold.

## XXX

When the music stops, when the wide-winged
shadows pass by, when breaths mingle
in the patience of the red rose and the dance
is motionless at last, when all the edges and hollows
are caught in the moment of change and cold air
fails empty and calm, let your hand take root in a world
in which you play no part, in the wandering scrawl
that remains when the sky is closed.
Rise up like a shout in an empty house.
Stand naked in front of the mirror.
You are revealed in every element and truth,
your face is drawn and marked on every wall.

## XXXI

The least motion, the vulnerable descent
at the beginning of winter
and the pale stones behind the barn
wet and bare under a half moon.
The sky smells of rain and dust
and the white oaks outside my window
hold on as the landscapes shift.
Alone that evening, the train gone,
I remembered your fragile hollows,
the stark shadows on the wall when you left,
the sudden light on the other side of the door,
the brittle scent of the air as I fell.

## XXXII

I reach no conclusions
in the foreign light, the day's boundaries
abstract and shattering to origins
and eddies in the rigid angles of night.
Rain echoes slowly in a high wind.
The simple attestations of a distant solution—
the broken heart begging to be healed—
spiraling out from the lost corners of October
until nothing remains, only the drift
of voices bent in the clear sweetness of air,
and a woman's body, deep as the earth,
shaken free at the edge of the sea.

## XXXIII

It was an artificial light
reflected on a curtained wall.
The continuum of stones muffled
against the white self
ledged in the requirements of the moment.
The sum of those events released
like scraps of old paper in the street,
the rain beginning changeless and particular
in the distance across the bridge,
and a quickened vision of isolation or love.
The clear line of the roof descends
on the other side of the setting sun.

## XXXIV

The well-lit room with two yellow vases
echoes with the sound of something
unexpected mounting the stairs.
Outside, in the hallway, love goes dry.
The street is full of old stars
and the ashes that outlined your face.
The night is endless and the mute sky shudders.
The day will be heavy after rain.
Time is swept away, vanishes among the dead stones.
The moon falls on the windows, works across
surfaces and lines I no longer remember.
Behind me, something whispers *lost fire*.

## XXXV

I woke late in the empty house,
the bare bones of the sky washed
to metal and stone overhead,
and watched dim shapes move across
the clouds as rain thickened to snow
and ice, swinging into unguent light.
The radiance of the day is without intention.
I am overcome with amazement
and fear falls away unclaimed.
Let the others down below run. I'll stay.
It keeps alive in darkness, in dust and air.
The pattern at last intends its own course.

## XXXVI

The responsibility of love realized
whispers something beautiful and old,
the perfect edge of a hand as it moves
across your face, constant and white,
and folds away as your body shifts,
a summer bird above the wilting flowers:
the sudden lines around your mouth,
the weightless stones gathered in mourning,
the thin light along the cold back stairs
and the shadow moving down the page:
the stub and halt of every horizon
as it quenches the changes of the moon.

## XXXVII

It was when the last bird flew by the window
wounded in the leg, its feathers a curse to be lifted
by a still wind and the sun's red crest as it slides
backwards to its fine collapse, that he stood an exile
in the streets, shadows anointing the cobblestones
to the deep gray glow where the dead preside.
It was a drifting across an inaccessible ledge
to a place of familiar wonders wide as a span of wings
and short as the pain of hands that draw away
to the cold fissures of dirt and distant truths.
The god of flowers sustains undone dances
and obscure visions, and the parted waters burn.

## XXXVIII

The stolen hours carried him beyond the lands
he surveyed, following the arches of the moon
hanging in the sky like a guarded mirror
that reflects horizons far and wide,
the high bridge of salvation that whispers his name
as the rains pass somewhere in the east
and float up across the garden's trance,
the nearest exit a periphery of space and light.
All this was out of reach: the hawk of redemption
freeing us one by one from the darkness of the world,
bent westward by the spears of miracle and sin.
The trees around us shift their inconsolate roots.

## XXXIX

Fish and flocks, the unsummoned image,
matter and form, the earth-brown core
of unbordered lands dreamed like the broken ghosts
of absolution as the branches spread.
The stitch no world can offer, the dream that holds
the last lease on time, the moment that swells
and dies, unwinding a spirit that will never fall.
And when he turned, the sea drew back into the river's
cold waters that cannot be crossed and whose sands never rest.
The two halves of the horseman of God broke the tunneled heart.
The stolen hour widened as infinity staggered the earth.
And the darkness, the darkness stayed alive.

## XL

The certain solitudes of the blood moon
drift through obstinate glass, lift the errors
of the blind man's eye. Everything changes
in spite of the light, the black marl of air
waiting to be moved across the bottom rung,
the blind interiors shuttered like blades in the dirt,
fading from dream to dream to attics and vague smoke.
At a time like this nothing suffices.
The horizon falls indifferently on the veranda.
Tomorrow is a warp of earth and myth.
The rapid pulse of orphaned hands
drums a miraculous escape, sibilant and black.

## XLI

We stepped across the broken glass
on the icy rocks and the tide stirred
skeletal and thin in the tethers of a colder day.
The weightless stone displaced the air
and time scatters, a thing of hunger,
to an innocent flutter of sand and dry seed
somewhere in the nameless folding of snow.
I make myself small in the dark grace ahead.
The waters recede and the lights
in the distance finally flicker out.
The white hills whisper: late winter.
The marrow cries: dead sea.

## XLII

The indifferent night writes an old history
in the corner of the room and dark clothes dry
in the moonlight like a memory of absent flowers.
She floats across the bare floor, arms open
to her own reflection in the window.
The city is frozen. The streetlights fail.
Something fills the passageways and makes
no sound as the season ends, descends
and circles the constellations overhead.
You will never sleep, wrapped in red blankets,
will stammer on all fours with unwelcome ghosts.
Outside, eyes closed, the future taps its stick.

## XLIII

Snow falls on old statues in the square,
the rumor of other storms drifting
across the empty spaces of the sky.
You stand in the doorway, a cold inclination,
lost in your own reasons and whirls.
The moon splits above the rooftops.
The curtains in the window fade.
A dry light from the attic falls in the street,
waits to be moved through the shadows
when the last doors close. The pale statues
watch their dreams end, the moment over
as darkness breaks, a sudden quiet in the air.

## XLIV

We each close a door to a small room
and the windows slide blindly into dusk.
We are each gone a little more each night,
backs pressed against cold walls,
bones folding upward across the ceilings
and drifting downward to asterisks of light.
There is no true measure, nothing past
the circles of hanging bulbs on bare floors,
the ending banked to a graceless touch.
The narrow orbit of the earth rounds
to a deep dead calm, the sharp profile
of the moon a small mercy that turns and slips.

## XLV

Day at last turns into night
and the small brink of the world
shifts directionless and grave
to a damask of lost voices,
a mosaic of fragments and shards
that folds across the immaculate hills,
a play of dense and faint light
weeping like the last embrace of death.
I go backwards in time, wind through
glass and air, return to where I rise and fall.
I lean forward in a world of slow dreams.
In the distance, a black dog howls.

## XLVI

Those old things that filled the room
move unexpectedly to a sudden indifference.
Memory keeps them the way they were,
half-hidden in a bodiless light,
as moments come and go without intention.
This is what it means when mirrors burn
like harsh wounds and the windows fill with ash,
when the deep crimson of time falls away
and I hear the cold smolder of broken shadows
faint across the corners of the crescent moon.
I listen hard for a long time.
The walls begin to whisper in the night.

XLVII

Endless clouds of smoke fill the horizon.
Night glows: embers of wood and charred bones.
Sleep: we press against each other and tremble,
morning somewhere far off around the corner.
I long for the one who is not here, I do not have.
I hold her wandering soul in my hand.
It moves like an old dream that hastens
to its quick delay, dark and secret in the dust.
The shadow in the hallway gathers like a gesture
in the small folds of the stairs.
The dreadful joy of the window blanches the floor.
The wall stands still in its own pale light.

## XLVIII

A heavy vine of wings covers the stones
scattered in the far left corner of the garden,
twilight gathering and the roads thinning
along the edges of the cleared fields,
a thousand knives cutting through the lost voices
of all the dead who lie in wait there forever.
Time blackens to the core of a great wheel
that turns without stop in the blood red water
and white words reconcile with the blind
lashings of the flat wide stars. Alongside,
a hesitant step. This place alone is my own,
my only measure however brief this light.

## XLIX

An abandoned child sleeps alone
in a nest of grass and wire.
I lift her, light as a bird, and coat
her in layers of wax and dust.
She floats between two suns, her hands
seeking what she already knows,
a single continuum, hollow as bone,
lost in its own long slide.
I dreamed of a bridge in a silent world,
saw the sad light of her eyes and low voice
floating like the present and the future
linked far below on the lucid water.

L

The weather changes, separating shadow and light.
Beyond the fence of vines and wild myrtle,
the hesitations of the coddled edge,
the interventions of a universe of lines,
the dead cedars of abstraction and grief.
He was not the last one home again,
birds whistling down the river, the blue haze
widening to deeper sounds, lifted up like the moon
in blind hands pressed against old windows:
I set fire to the deep roots, watched the long grasses
vanish on the hill, coaxed the stars at last awake—
the eastern sky full of the dark, of me.

## LI

The curve around the bend in the road
speaks in a flat voice, staggers to its feet
on a slant of wind in a sleepless dawn.
When I stand upright as the rains fall
like dropped coins begged in the street
across from the closed doors of old houses,
my bones turn to feathers and wild leaves,
the sympathetic colors of some more distant
source of light taking root in the grim speed
of roses blue as slate as they open and burn.
In three days they will rise again to time and light.
I will stay the quick dust I was made to be.

## LII

At the other edge of the field, toward the end of May,
just before the sun rises and the season fully changes,
an unexpected fog roots itself among the poplars,
dangling loose across the empty places in the grass,
caught and held for hours, and then drifting
to the still light that holds the world together.
It is a perfection of motion, a moving brilliance,
a secret beyond the silent corners of the sky,
the old contours of my life forgotten somewhere.
It would not move through the cold bones of my hand,
would not whisper to ghosts when the moon went black.
Forgive me. I dreamed your death, the paling of red stones.

## LIII

The rage of summer fires in the distance,
the sky layered with patterns of smoke that paw
the dry shadows overhead, the pointed stick of time
scratching its thin lines across the horizon,
and a woman who cannot speak walking beside me.
The palm of her hand tasted like the sea,
water that rises on the wind from a hard lake.
Pale images in her pale hair darkened as a white streak
of soundless birds creased through the brush,
stirred ashes rising into an afternoon of ripples and weeds.
The day, one wing broken, coils round itself into night.
Look: your name glows white in the burned grass ahead.

## LIV

Winter is hanging on, a cold fire.
I rise up out of the snow, following
my own shadow, and burrow sunlight
all evening in my arms, looking for
something simple and familiar under
the roots of the dead sycamore.
Everything is silent here, drifting
face down in the clouds, the light pitiless
and close to the quick of evening.
I hear the owl settling into the furrows
of the dark barn, the spider climbing
along the numb spine of the far wall.

## LV

Evening offers no relief. The incandescence
of late afternoon continues to smooth the blood
and the black birds in the tangle of trees
across the way dream of the last white shadows.
The woman who was weeping, who loved me
all this time, belongs to someone else.
When I close my eyes, I see her walking up
the long back stairs, waiting to be touched,
see the hand that floats away on the blind air,
the breath that thrives on longing, the door
that shuts forever under the unpredictable moon.
White shadows huddle together, dreaming of birds.

LVI

The broken boxes the moon fell into last night
were kicked down the center of the street
by the wings of horned owls hunting for the promise
of obscured things, the slow fade of lost words
fumbling in a cauldron of cold air,
the tiny bones spinning secrets in the white ground.
The doors close when an unborn child dies.
Stone walls shift their lenses down through
the bewildered formalities of time and winter.
The sky shatters the isolated bridge.
The rattle of old leaves lifts the world to tears.
The radiance of vacant boundaries says nothing.

LVII

The rituals of time mock the rigid stars.
In the opaque mist, dun-colored birds bind the sky
for hours, sift through the halves of light
shifting in the banded water, the synthesis
of loosened day and endless night.
In the distance, yellow light falls from a window,
lenient and old, and the half-buried moans of dry wind
across the roofline are brittle as burned grass.
My broken soul leans back against its hour,
startling itself in the absence of sound and air.
I am at the center, released from form.
The pall of infinity tilts. Desire broods.

## LVIII

The private certainties of time, when the tide
flocks against cold stones and night lengthens,
rootless and ridged, against the hollows
of a safer ground, are caught by chance in circles
of black water and grow opaque as bone,
mute smoke and dust dancing in dead air,
the abrupt landscape insolvent in its ebb and flow.
It will be like this when I die: breaking loose
on a high wind from the vacancies of this place.
Now, the small town past the bridge outwits the day.
Far below, small folds and footprints in empty sand.
The final grace of a brief and running light.

## LIX

The last white leaf on the birch tree as the storm passes
recovers in the muted shadows of a secret light.
The wind off the water quickens to a drift of gray,
the sound of darkness moving slow and alone
through the creviced roots, and the long
low waves gather the river to its banks.
At the high window, watching the air scrub
the moving stones along the far lines of the yard,
I thought I saw your face in the glass,
your hands falling empty as the angel wheeled past.
One feather of one wing plumbed the night:
I am afraid of the dark, of the earth as it spins.

## LX

The river gathered itself quickly near the fallen trees
and the black ridge narrowed to roots and deaf stones
at the field's closed edge, its somber hands opening
the flat hard landscape where bodies rise from the dead.
The stars have gone to brown water, sad and beautiful,
and a lost skirt lies on the ground near the low ring
of dry weeds by the last still bend in the road.
The day grows old. God's gray hand touches my face.
Through the walls, the last lament, huddled like a mute bell,
echoes in a fold of sad feathers and bones.
Wait for me. I'll come home when the shadows slip below.
We will rise together, soar back into summer light.

*Afterword: Notes on the Paintings and Poems*

    I began thinking about writing the poems in this collection one afternoon a few years ago while standing in one of the galleries at the New Britain Museum of American Art, where I have been visiting for some fifty years, and looking once again at *McVey's Barn* by Andrew Wyeth. I had seen that painting for the first time as a teenager and was so moved by it then that I wrote a poem, which I admit from this distance in time seems at best rudimentary, to make permanent for myself the astonishing immersion into that piece that I felt while standing before it, absorbing and breathing in its beckoning textures and probing light. I tried, in that early poem, to report my experience, to see if words could recreate my love of that painting, as a visual appreciation and recitation as well as an emotional jolt. I have that poem secure in its anonymity in a closed folder, along with other poems written when I was seventeen. Next to it also is a poem I wrote about seeing that painting again seventeen years later, when I found myself back in that museum after all those years had passed. It is a different kind of poem, layered in a different way, reflecting on the painting, of course, but now seeking not to report on it or on my experience seeing it but instead committed to creating a parallel experience, springboarding from Wyeth more deeply into myself and exploring in that self, as I then knew it, the meanings and significances of the profound sense of loss Wyeth depicts.

    I have thought often since those two essential and special

moments, separated by the years, in front of that painting, about how seeing the piece affected me not just as a visitor to the gallery who is in some way touched by the works he is seeing but as someone who wishes to capture and present—or perhaps re-present—how and why he has been affected. For me, that had something to do with being an observer as well as a reciprocal participant, engaging and being engaged by the wonderful and often overwhelmingly beautiful objects and colors and shadings of brushstroke and line in front of me. Over the years, I've decided that such engagements—across the world and across our lives, and not just linking to works of art but in and through all those special connections that provide insight and revelation—are moments of epiphany. I don't necessarily mean that in a theological sense, though some of that element is part of my understanding of that idea and present in some of the poems in these pages. I mean, rather, an intense and often startling experience, a sudden and deeply powerful realization of significance and meaning, of the thing seen and of the effect felt or understood.

These "epiphanic moments" provide, for me, a sense of revelation of the pinpoint of experience, in its most immediate expression. That experience is usually free of narrative progression but not necessarily free of the concentric circles of the considered moment, that is, of all the horizontal details of such a moment. There is a story to be told, but it is a story that does not unfold over time but exists in that lightning flash. My goal in writing these poems is to see if I can create those moments, to use and engage what I consider to be the painterly qualities of language, of image and metaphor, and to consider each word within the poem as part of an overlaying of lines and images, as individual strokes of the brush. The epiphanic moments I am interested in exploring in these pages have something to do with such layerings of the world and with the act of unfolding those layers, not to define progression to some conclusion but to encourage immediacy of connection and insight, perhaps much like the experience I had standing in front of *McVey's Barn*. So in these poems I have worked to create layers, some overlapping the way stones often overlap in piles, and to do so with the hope that in that act of creation I could ask the reader to see simplicity in texture and, in like fashion, complexity in the simple resonances of words and lines. That may be the essential task of the lyric poem, and I consider these poems lyric in that way.

As I was thinking about this book, in the Museum, I knew that this gathering of poems would be immensely enriched by the kind of parallel artistic experience I had when writing that second poem about Wyeth's painting. That has something to do with my belief in the reverberant connections between and among works of art, in various genres and forms. All artists, no matter their foundational materials, explore similar themes, and I believed that the epiphanic moments I am interested in would generate new engaging energy through a collaboration with a painter who had a profound understanding of those resonances and who could create not a commentary on my poems but an experience of equal valence. Only one person came to mind: the extraordinary painter, poet, philosopher Steven Schroeder. During the course of the past decade, I have had the joyful privilege of reading his magisterial poetry, celebrating his astonishing paintings, and thinking with him about how and why art, in all its forms, makes us human and alive. His paintings, as the sequence he has created here so beautifully shows, live in a world of insight and revelation. They are autonomous comments on some of the images my poems explore, but more than that they are in and of themselves epiphanies, in each striking element, in each texture and image, in each subtle turn, drawing us into a resonant moment, into the very heart of truth.

    I am privileged to have worked with Steve on this book. Our collaboration has been a remarkably satisfying and essential literary experience for me. Regina Schroeder's masterful presentation of our collaboration brings the works, and all of us, together in art.

*Jonas Zdanys*
*Wallingford and New Britain*
*February 2016*

Over the years that I've had the pleasure of knowing and working with Jonas Zdanys, I've often thought of him not only as a poet but also as a painter whose chosen medium is the written word. *Red Stones* reflects this at every turn in poems that embody what he refers to as "the epiphanic moment" in lyric poetry. I share Jonas's fascination with such moments, so I was delighted when he invited me to paint with him in this collection.

I had encountered a number of the poems before—in *Cormorants*, in the *Wonderbook of Poetry*, and in *all roads will lead you home*—so I came to the whole ready to dwell on familiar spaces in new light. It's important, I think, that the phrase Jonas uses to name the driving force of these poems combines a matter of light (epiphany) with a bit of time (the moment), a combination that is critical to lyric poetry. Dwelling on them, as one does in the close reading that is part of a collaboration like this, adds an experience of space we all know as embodied beings. Whatever we set out to do takes place; and, in the process of doing it, we make places. And that is worthy of reflection.

I'd like to think this place is more like a studio in which we work together than a gallery in which we put our work on display. In this case, Jonas paints with words while I paint with pigment. And, recalling the times Regina (whose medium is paper and print) and I painted together when she was young (and how we never painted the same thing no matter what was right before our eyes), I think it is worth noting that you will find three painters working when you enter this studio.

One effect of recognizing that Jonas and I are painting together is to remove any lingering temptation to illustrate the poems. We have made a shared space in which to paint, but we have not painted at the same time in the same light with the same thing in mind (even when what we've had in mind was nothing). And that may shed some light on how dwelling together over time makes a place that has a character that is distinctive and may be interesting.

I wrote earlier of close reading. For me, that took the form of reading the poems again and again before I painted and as I painted. In the process, I found images that caught my eye and often brought other images to mind. In painting, I followed as many as I could, knowing that one thing leads to another. When Jonas wrote of a blue dream paling in a flat land, I responded to a paling I knew in my bones from the Texas Panhandle and South Plains. And the long yellow grass in my mind's eye was the tall grass of the prairie that stretches across the Flint Hills of Kansas and the Osage Hills of Oklahoma into the Texas Panhandle. Every time I turned over a red stone, I saw shale cliffs, thought of Wichita River mud, and heard red dirt music. And the trees with their tangled roots were made more vivid by the memory of their absence. I found myself reading "alder" and thinking "mesquite." And that took me back to my father including a little bit of mesquite in the harp he made for Regina before he died. Mesquite is a tonewood. But that's another story...

Part of my fascination with epiphany is how consistently

it defies containment. It seems to me that the poems in this collection (and lyric poems more generally when they work) don't contain epiphanic moments so much as they are such moments. And one beauty of moments like that when you dwell on them is that they take you places you have never been, places that surprise you.

As I write this, I don't know what Regina will make of the book—but I look forward to it, as I look forward to seeing what the place becomes when you enter.

The studio is open. There is work to be done. Welcome.

*Steven Schroeder*
*Chicago*
*February 2016*

I always have to laugh when people ask me to talk about my "design process." Remember, one of the conventions of good design is Beatrice Ward's crystal goblet—it should be invisible. There are, of course, other schools of thought on the matter, but I love working in the background, so it works for me. It's why I played organ, it's why I prefer organizing to answering phones, it's probably why I'm a goalie, it's why I design books instead of writing them.

So: here's my process. Thirty-plus years of looking at books. Thirty-plus years of making images. More than a decade absorbing specific conventions of typography and studying the details of typefaces. A few years of engaging with the physicality of making texts, printing from metal type on presses from the wooden common press of Franklin, to the iron handpress of the nineteenth century newspaper, to the proofing presses of the mid-twentieth century. Constantly thinking about proportions, line length, visual relationships.

Add to that some intense contemplation of the physical components of books—the paper, the glue, the stitching of a fine hardcover—and you arrive at a place where you can make a book in your head. Take it all, put it together, make it disappear.

It doesn't always work quite the way you think it's going to, of course—you learn new things about margins every time, and it takes a while to learn to translate what something looks like on a computer's monitor to what it will look like with different means of production.

That's what you're always striving towards: a book that doesn't interfere with the text, placement of images and titles that enlightens rather than clouds, and that will be pleasant to the reader's eye whether or not they know precisely why.

*Regina Schroeder*
*Malden*
*February 2016*

STEVEN SCHROEDER is a poet and visual artist who was born in Wichita Falls, grew up in the Texas Panhandle, studied at Valparaiso University and the University of Chicago, and spent many years moonlighting as a professor of philosophy and religious studies in Indiana, Iowa, Ohio, Wisconsin, Shenzhen, and Chicago (after a stint in community organizing and social work in Amarillo and Pampa). He has written, co-written, or edited thirty books (though some readers have concluded that it's really thirty variations on a single book). Still fine tuning, he has a new collection of poems (*the moon, not the finger, pointing*), published by Lamar University Literary Press in 2016. More at stevenschroeder.org

JONAS ZDANYS is a bilingual poet and translator who was born in New Britain, Connecticut, shortly after his parents arrived in the United States from a United Nations camp for Lithuanian refugees. He is the author of forty-four other books, forty of them collections of his own poetry, written in English and in Lithuanian, and of his translations of Lithuanian literature. He has received a number of prizes, book awards, writing and travel grants, and public recognitions for his own poetry and for his translations. He has taught at the State University of New York and at Yale University, where he also held a number of administrative positions and was a Scholar-in-Residence in the Yale Center for Russian and East European Studies. He served for more than a decade as the state of Connecticut's Chief Academic Officer and is currently Professor of English and Poet-in-Residence at Sacred Heart University, where he teaches seminars on modern poetry and directs the program in creative writing. More at http://jonaszdanys.org/

REGINA SCHROEDER does design to fuel her hockey habit, and has produced a tidy pile of poetry, prose, and exhibition catalogs for various authors and visual artists. She tells people she was raised by anarcho-syndicalist wolves in the wilds of Chicago, which is only a little untrue. She works in anachronistic media whenever possible, but is always happy to investigate contemporary methods when those serve her purpose. Of late, her work has been primarily in design with forays into fiber. She hasn't done anything on the internet in over a year, so her website is hopelessly out of date.

## Image Credits

*Angels Made of Straw (Title Page)*
watercolor, ink, and acrylic on paper, 20x14 inches [2015]
*The Last White Leaf (Contents)*
watercolor, ink, and acrylic on paper, 14x20 inches [2016]
*White Shadows (0)*
watercolor, ink, and acrylic on paper [2015]
*Blue Dream Paling 2 (6-7)*
oil on hardboard, 48x24 inches [2015]
*Long Yellow Grass (14)*
oil on canvas, 24x36 inches [2016]
*Black Alders Gray Water (22)*
watercolor on paper, 14x20 inches [2016]
*White Burns (32-33)*
watercolor and acrylic on paper, 20x14 inches [2015]
*White Moon Pausing (44-45)*
oil on canvas, 36x24 inches [2016]
*Revelations of Old Walls (51, cover)*
watercolor, ink, and acrylic on paper, 14x20 inches [2015]
*White Burns in Pitch Black (55)*
ink and acrylic on paper, 14x20 inches [2016]
*A World In Gray (59)*
watercolor, ink, and acrylic on paper, 14x20 inches [2015]
*Red Stones (63)*
watercolor on paper, 14x20 inches [2016]
*Water Circles (70)*
watercolor and acrylic on paper, 14x20 inches [2015]
*A Source of Constant Light 2 (74-75)*
oil on hardboard, 48x24 inches [2015]

www.ingramcontent.com/pod-product-compliance
Lightning Source LLC
Chambersburg PA
CBHW050817090426
42736CB00022B/3481